9
11
13
15

Add
17
Maestoso (♩ = 75)
molto legato
22
26
31
Reduce
Reduce

36
Ch. Trumpet
Gt.
3
40
(♮)
44
48
3
Gt.

52
Reduce
piú mosso (♩ = 98)
Reduce
Reduce
Reduce
57
Gt. Flute 8', 4', 2⅔', 2', 1⅗', Tremolo
Sw. Flute 8', 4'
61
65

69
74
79
Gt. Principal 8', 4'
Add
cresc. poco a poco
Gt.
accelerando
84
Add
Add
molto rit.

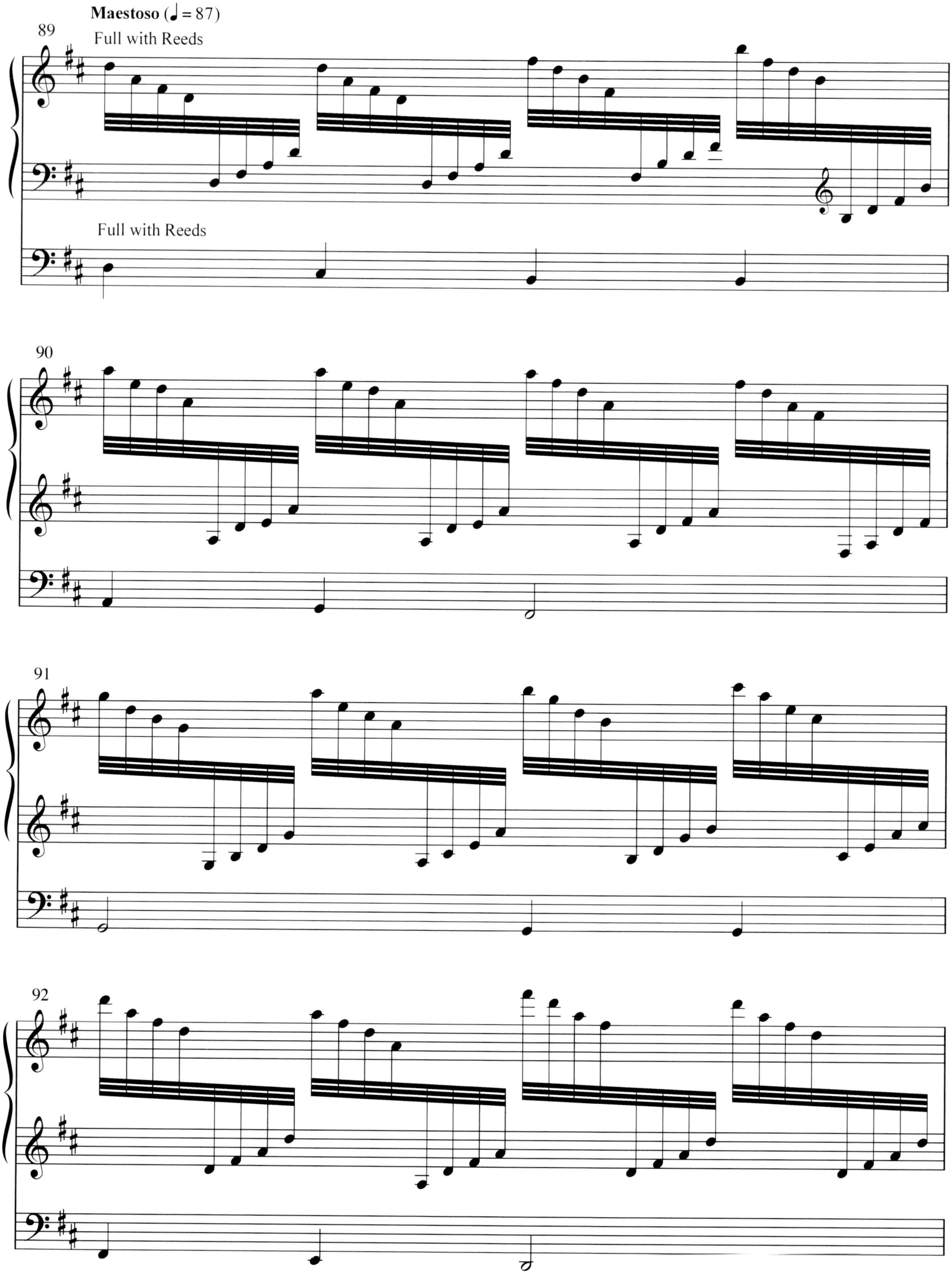
Maestoso (♩ = 87)
89
Full with Reeds
Full with Reeds
90
91
92

93
94
95
96

97
98
99
100
poco a poco rit.